ULTIMATE PLAY-
Just CLASSIC JAZZ

MW01041949

Project Manager: Aaron Stang
Performance Notes and Additional Text by Doug Munro
Guitar Solos Transcribed by Danny Begelman
Engraver: Adrian Alvarez
Technical Editor: Jack Allen
Text Editor: Nadine DeMarco
Art Design: Ken Rehm
Cover Guitar: Benedetto "Kenny Burrell Model Prototype" Courtesy of Cindy Benedetto
Photo by Ronald Chicken

WARNER BROS. PUBLICATIONS
Warner Music Group
An AOL Time Warner Company
USA: 15800 NW 48th Avenue, Miami, FL 33014

INTERNATIONAL MUSIC PUBLICATIONS LIMITED

ENGLAND: GRIFFIN HOUSE,
161 HAMMERSMITH ROAD, LONDON W6 8BS

© 2002 WARNER BROS. PUBLICATIONS
All Rights Reserved

Any duplication, adaptation or arrangement of the compositions
contained in this collection requires the written consent of the Publisher.
No part of this book may be photocopied or reproduced in any way without permission.
Unauthorized uses are an infringement of the U.S. Copyright Act and are punishable by law.

CONTENTS

Some Other Time

I tried to get some independence between the changes and melody on this song. It is probably one of the easier songs to play and solo over. I've always liked to use chord voicings that incorporate open strings because of the way they ring out so nicely. The A section has that open G string in the voicings so you get the sound of a pedal-tone going under the melody.

You'll find a great recording of this piece on Bill Evans' *The Village Vanguard Sessions* (two-record set) with Bill Evans on piano, Scott LaFaro on bass, and Paul Motian on drums. This was originally recorded on the Milestone record label in 1961. You should also check out Bill Evans' studio-recorded version on his CD *Waltz for Debbie*.

The Song

- This song has a 32-bar AABA form. Each section is eight bars in length.
- The three A sections are in C major.
- The bridge, or B section, is in Ab major.
- The second A section ends with a II-V modulation (Bbm7-Eb7) to the new key of Ab major.
- The bridge, or B section, has a tritone chord sub on the third beat of the measure [Amaj7(b5) instead of Bbm7-Eb7].
- In the chord-melody there is extensive use of scale-tone chords to harmonize the melody notes. (For example, the sixth bar of the last A section has Dm7-Em7-Fmaj7-G7sus as opposed to the original Dm7-G7.)

The Solo

- The solo has a double-time feel to it. (Note that the transcribed solo is twice as long as the head, with each section being 16 bars in length instead of eight.)
- The phrasing in this solo is always *across* the bar line, and the phrases never start on beat 1. This creates rhythmic tension, strong swing, and a good forward momentum for the solo.
- ..ere is a classic blues riff in bar 4 of the first A section.
- B..rs 15 and 16 of the first A section have a sixteenth-note sequential pattern that drives to the A section.
- The solo concludes with a return to the original feel leading to the B section.

Selected Recordings

Bill Evans, *Waltz for Debbie—Limited Edition*, JVC Victor.

Bill Evans, *Bill Evans and Tony Bennett*, Fantasy Original Jazz Classics, 1975.

Jackie McLean, *New York Calling*, 1994.

Mark Whitfield, *Forever Love*, UNI Verve, 1997.

SOME OTHER TIME
(Chord-Melody Solo)

Words by BETTY COMDEN
and ADOLPH GREEN
Music by LEONARD BERNSTEIN

© 1945 (Renewed) WARNER BROS. INC.
All Rights Reserved

SOME OTHER TIME
(Solo)

Words by BETTY COMDEN
and ADOLPH GREEN
Music by LEONARD BERNSTEIN

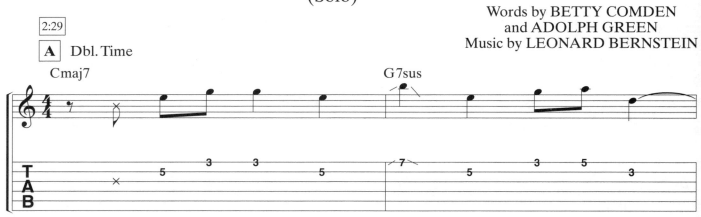

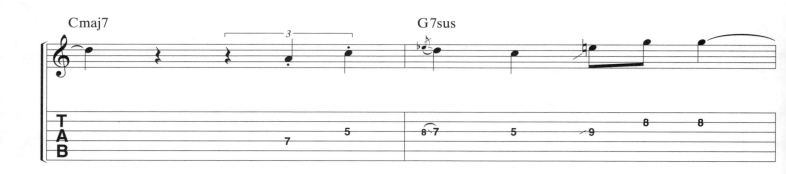

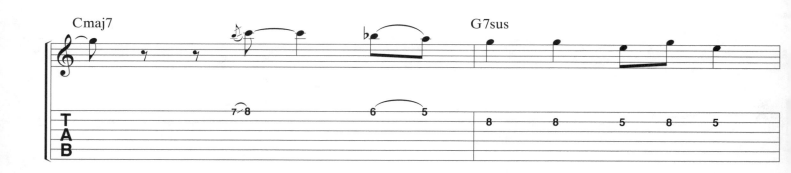

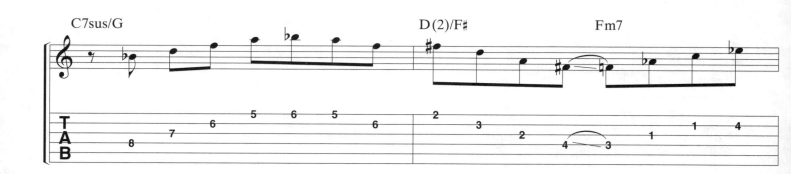

© 1945 (Renewed) WARNER BROS. INC.
All Rights Reserved

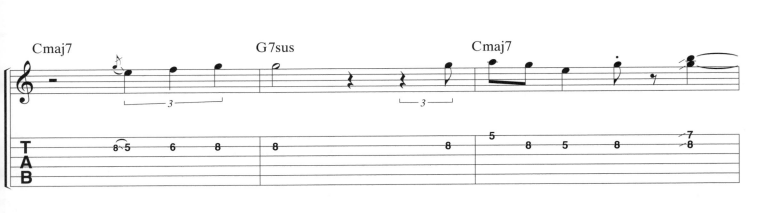

10

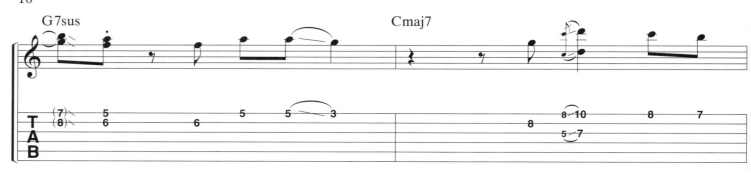

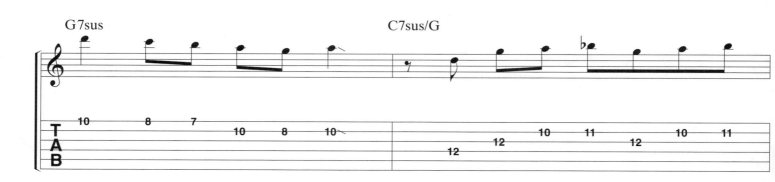

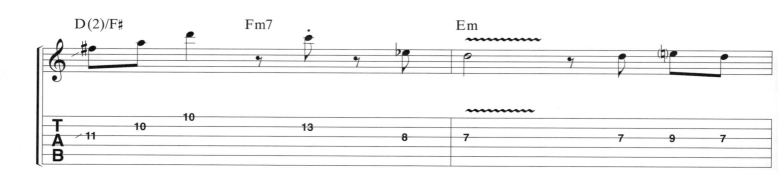

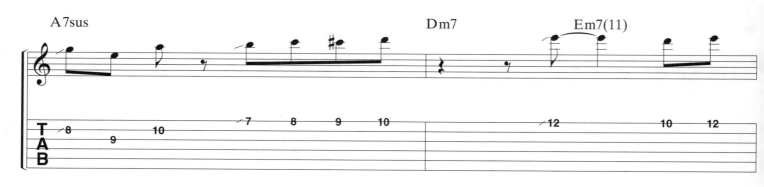

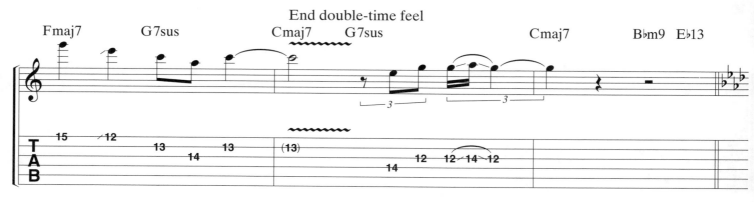

SOME OTHER TIME
(Original Fakebook Version)

Words by BETTY COMDEN
and ADOLPH GREEN
Music by LEONARD BERNSTEIN

© 1945 (Renewed) WARNER BROS. INC.
All Rights Reserved

0615B

Alone Together

Check out the form and the minor progressions throughout this piece. The last two bars (bars 11 and 12 of letter A) are a little different every time, which makes it more of an interesting progression.

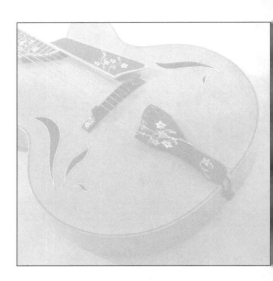

The chord voicings used in this piece are a bit unusual but not difficult to interpret. For the soloing, you are mainly in D minor or D harmonic minor (which gives you the C♯ for the A dominant chords). On the bridge you can use a C melodic minor and an E melodic minor for the A7(♭5), and E♭ melodic minor for the D7(♭5) resolving to the G minor scale. Then, the same thing happens again down a whole-step. You can use the B♭ melodic minor and/or the D melodic minor scale for the G7(♭5), and the D♭ melodic minor for the C7(♭5).

Check out a nice version of this song on a 1955 recording by tenor saxophonist Al Cohn entitled *The Jazz Workshop—Four Brass, One Tenor* on the RCA label.

The Song

- This song has a 44-bar AABA form. The first two A sections are 14 bars each. The B section and the last A section are eight bars each.
- The first two A sections are in D minor but resolve to D major at the end of each section.
- The bridge, or B section, has the same chord progression as the bridge of Dizzy Gillespie's "A Night in Tunisia." It is a series of II-V's, first in G minor and then in F major.
- The last A section differs from the first two A sections in its length (eight bars as opposed to 14), and its resolution (it stays in D minor as opposed to resolving to D major).

The Solo

- The solo is a mostly eighth-note swing solo with triplets used sparingly.
- The melody is hinted at in bars 3 and 5 and is strongly stated at the end of the solo.
- The playing has a strong harmonic quality because of the extensive use of arpeggio lines.
- In bar 13 of the first A section, the solo lands on the third (F♯) of the D major chord to reinforce the harmony.
- The second A section starts with a strong blues riff, which propels the solo forward.

- The D major harmony is presented in fourths at the end of the second A section.
- The last A section has the most aggressive rhythmic statement (the sixteenth-note sequence in bar 2).

Selected Recordings

Chet Baker, *1955–56: In Paris Barclay Sessions*, UNI Verve, 2000.

Miles Davis, *Milestones*.

Paul Desmond, *Take Ten*, BMG/RCA, 1978.

Dizzy Gillespie, *Groovin' High*, compilation release on Jazz Hour/NET, 2000.

Jazz Messengers, *Café Bohemia*, Part 1, Giants of Jazz (ITA), 1999.

Benedetto "La Cremona Fiorita," photo by Ronald Chicken, courtesy of Cindy Benedetto

ALONE TOGETHER
(Chord-Melody Solo)

Words by HOWARD DIETZ
Music by ARTHUR SCHWARTZ

© 1932 WARNER BROS. INC. Copyright Renewed
Rights for the Extended Renewal Term in the United States Controlled by
WARNER BROS. INC. and ARTHUR SCHWARTZ MUSIC
All Rights Reserved

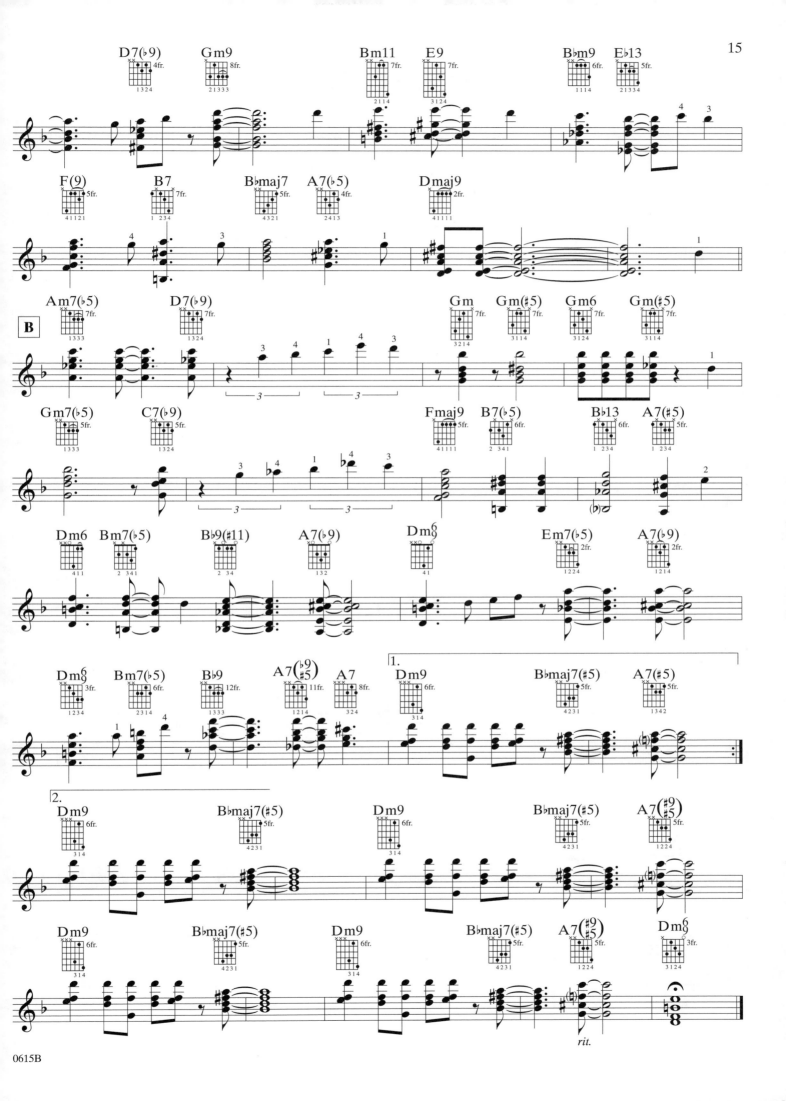

ALONE TOGETHER
(Solo)

Words by HOWARD DIETZ
Music by ARTHUR SCHWARTZ

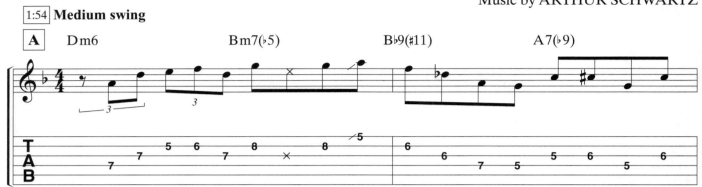

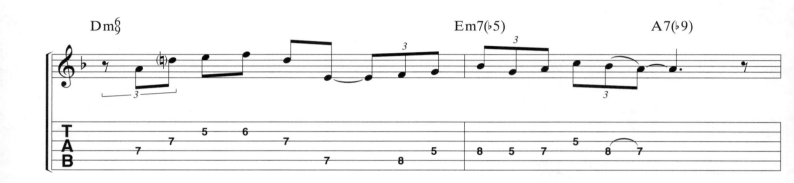

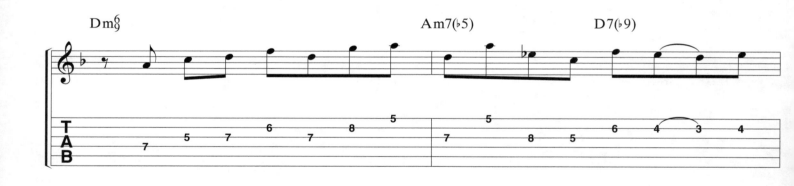

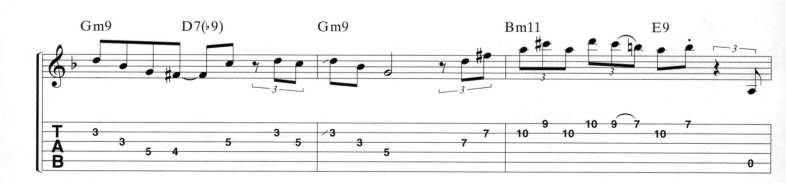

© 1932 WARNER BROS. INC. Copyright Renewed
Rights for the Extended Renewal Term in the United States Controlled by
WARNER BROS. INC. and ARTHUR SCHWARTZ MUSIC
All Rights Reserved

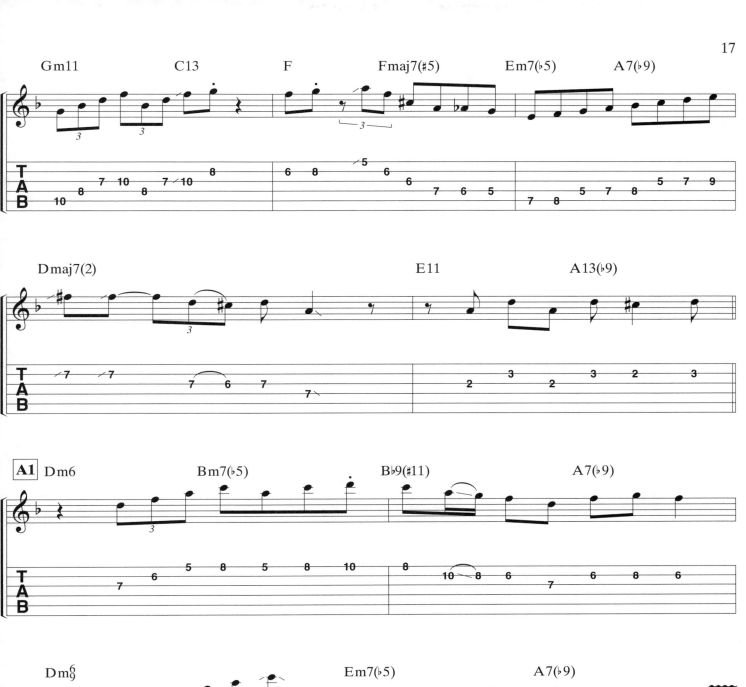

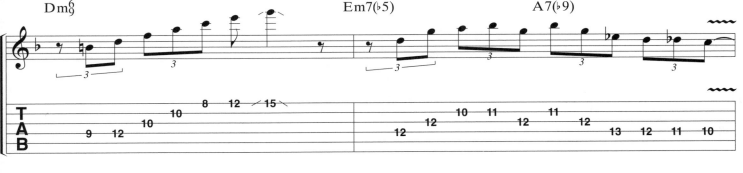

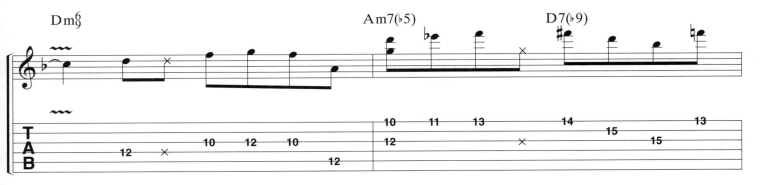

0615B

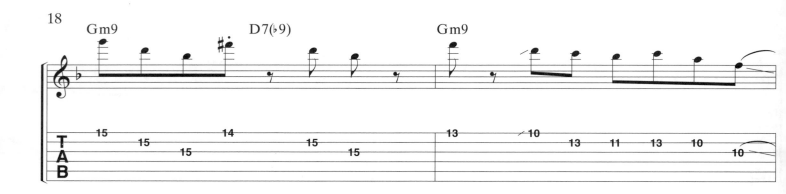

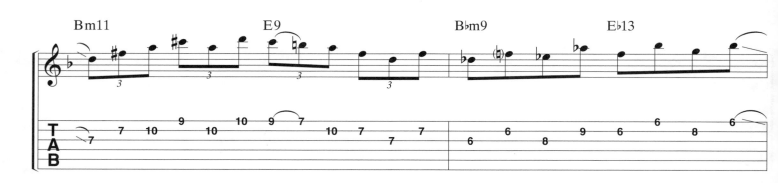

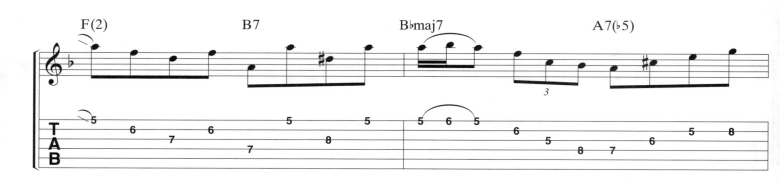

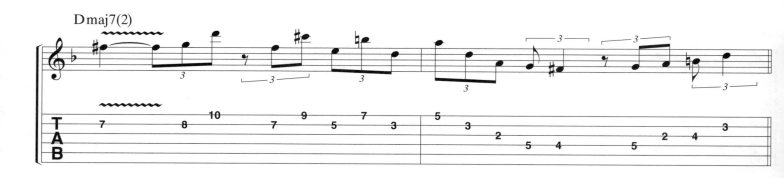

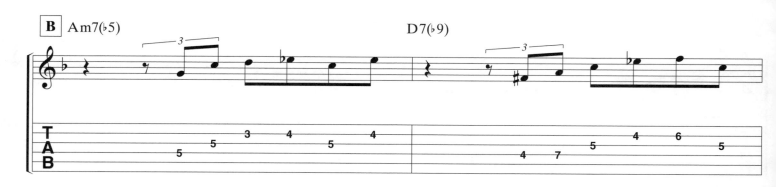

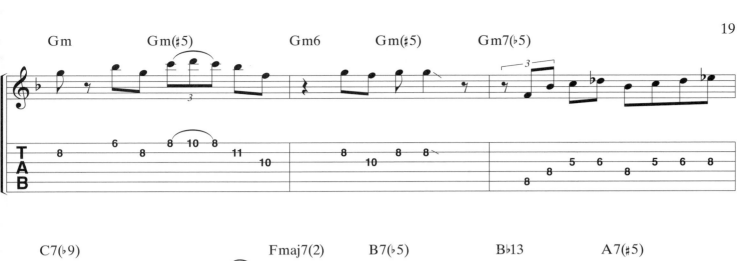

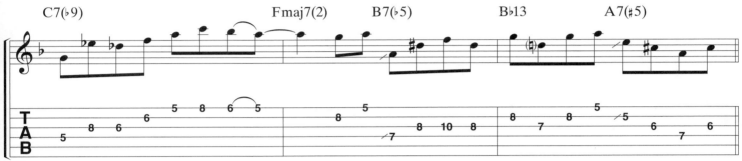

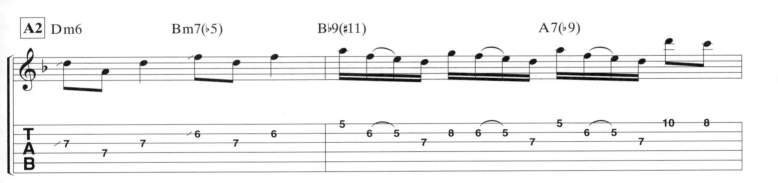

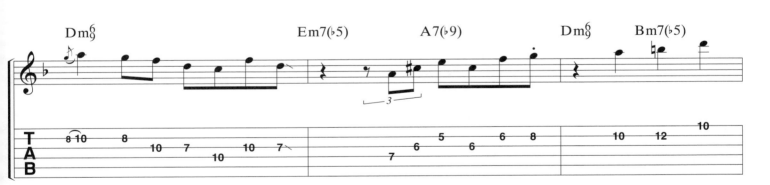

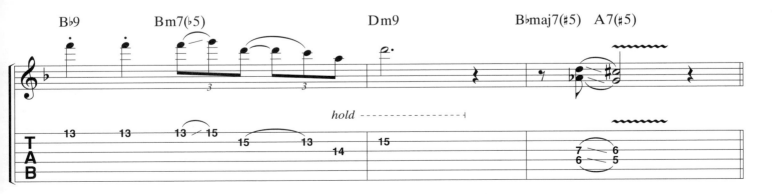

0615B

ALONE TOGETHER
(Original Fakebook Version)

Words by HOWARD DIETZ
Music by ARTHUR SCHWARTZ

Ballad or medium swing

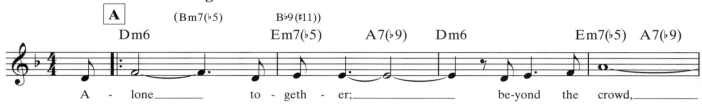

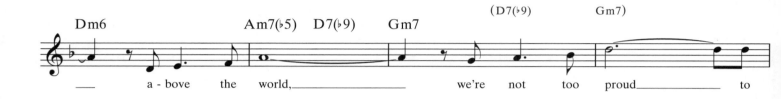

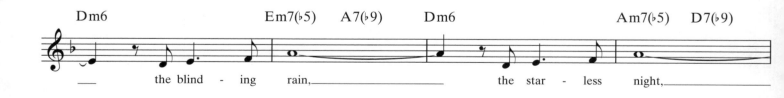

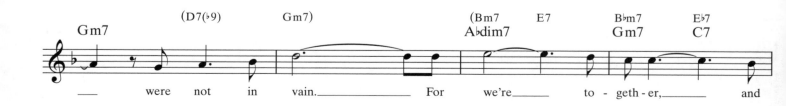

© 1932 WARNER BROS. INC. Copyright Renewed
Rights for the Extended Renewal Term in the United States Controlled by
WARNER BROS. INC. and ARTHUR SCHWARTZ MUSIC
All Rights Reserved

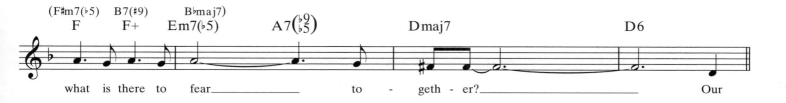

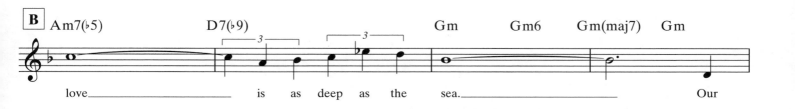

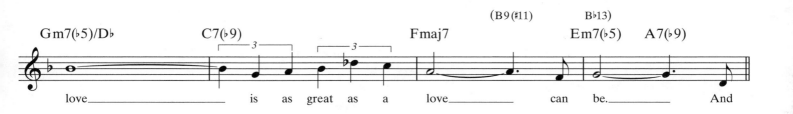

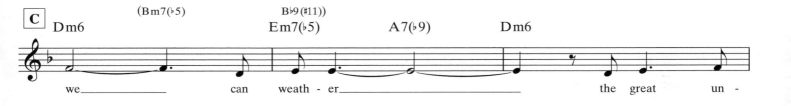

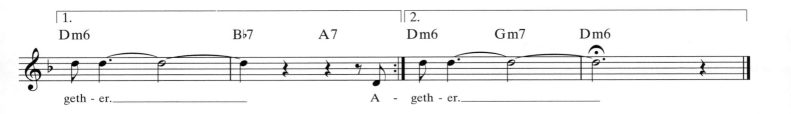

April in Paris

This song has an interesting yet tricky rhythmic element since many of the phrases end on the fourth beat of the bar. It can make a good exercise in keeping your place within the groove.

Notice the melody starting on bar 17 of letter A. Bars 17–24 are the most difficult to perform, and I suggest zeroing in and practicing these bars with a metronome. It will pay off and make the rest of the song easier in comparison.

There are many II-V progressions to maneuver through, with a minor 7(♭5) as the II chord. You can definitely use a major scale against those chords. For example, use an E♭ major scale for the Dm7(♭5) chord:

Dm7(♭5):	D		F		A♭		C	
E♭ Major:	D	E♭	F	G	A♭	B♭	C	D	E♭
		1	2	3	4	5	6	7	8

Jimmy Haslip found a great version by one of his favorite pianists, Errol Garner, on a recording entitled *Concert by the Sea* on the Columbia label, 1956, with Eddie Calhoun on bass and Denzil Best on drums.

Also try to find this wonderful recording of this piece by Thad Jones, *The Magnificent Thad Jones*, Blue Note, 1956.

The Song

- This song has a 32-bar A-A1-B-A2 form. Each section is eight bars long.
- The first A section is centered around a C major tonality with strong harmonic hints of C minor [for example, the Fm in bar 1 and the Dm7(♭5) in bar 3].
- The second A section (A1) goes through a series of brief tonal centers (F major, A minor, E minor) with a finale harmonic push in the eighth bar to the first chord of the B section (Dm) through Em7(♭5) and A7(♭9).
- The first four bars of the bridge, or B section, are again centered around a C major resolution with strong C minor overtones.
- The second half of the B section moves through two key centers (A minor and E major) and then II-V's back to the Fm chord of the last A section (A2).
- The last A section is centered around the same C minor and major resolutions with a stop off at the dominant six chord (A7) in bar 4.

The Solo

- The solo has numerous melody quotes (bars 1 and 3 of the A section; bars 3 and 5 of the A1 section; and bars 5 and 6 of the A2 section).
- There are scale-based passages (for example, bars 6 and 8 of the A section).
- There is a blues-style turn at the end of bar 3 into bar 4 in the B section.

Selected Recordings

Count Basie, *April in Paris*, UNI/Verve, 1955.

Clifford Brown, *Jazz 'Round Midnight*, re-issue UNI/Verve, 1993.

Miles Davis, *Conception*, import

Coleman Hawkins, *Body and Soul*, BMG/RCA Victor, 1939.

Billie Holiday, *Lady Sings the Blues*, reissue, 1998.

Barney Kessel, *Easy Like*, Fantasy/ Original Jazz Classics, 1953.

Gibson ES 165, "Herb Ellis" Model, courtesy of Gibson USA

APRIL IN PARIS
(Chord-Melody Solo)

Words by E. Y. HARBURG
Music by VERNON DUKE

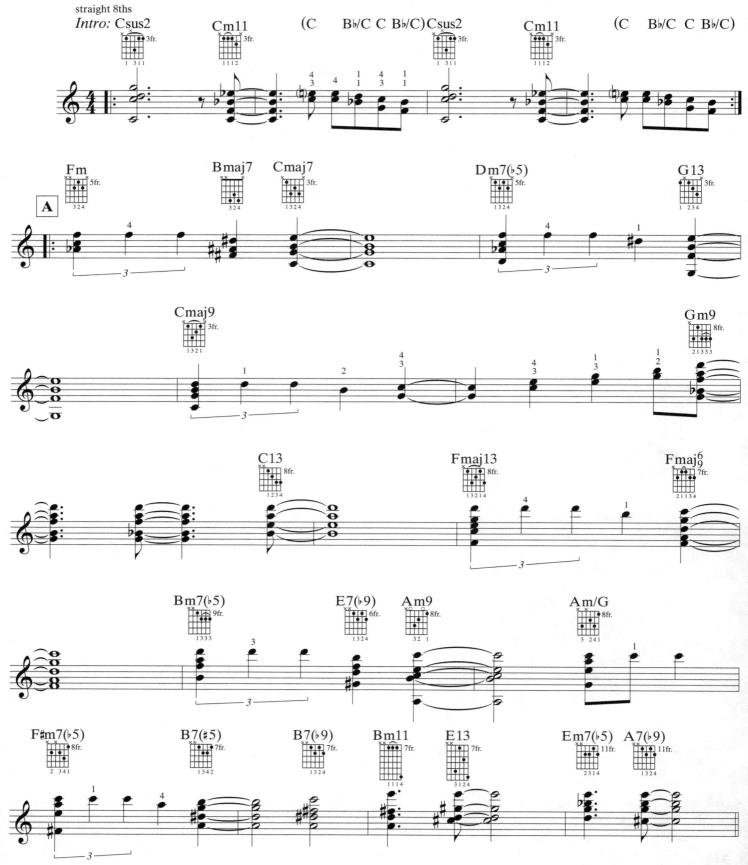

© 1932 WARNER BROS. INC.
Rights for the Extended Renewal Term in the United States Controlled by
GLOCCA MORRA MUSIC and KAY DUKE MUSIC
All Rights Reserved

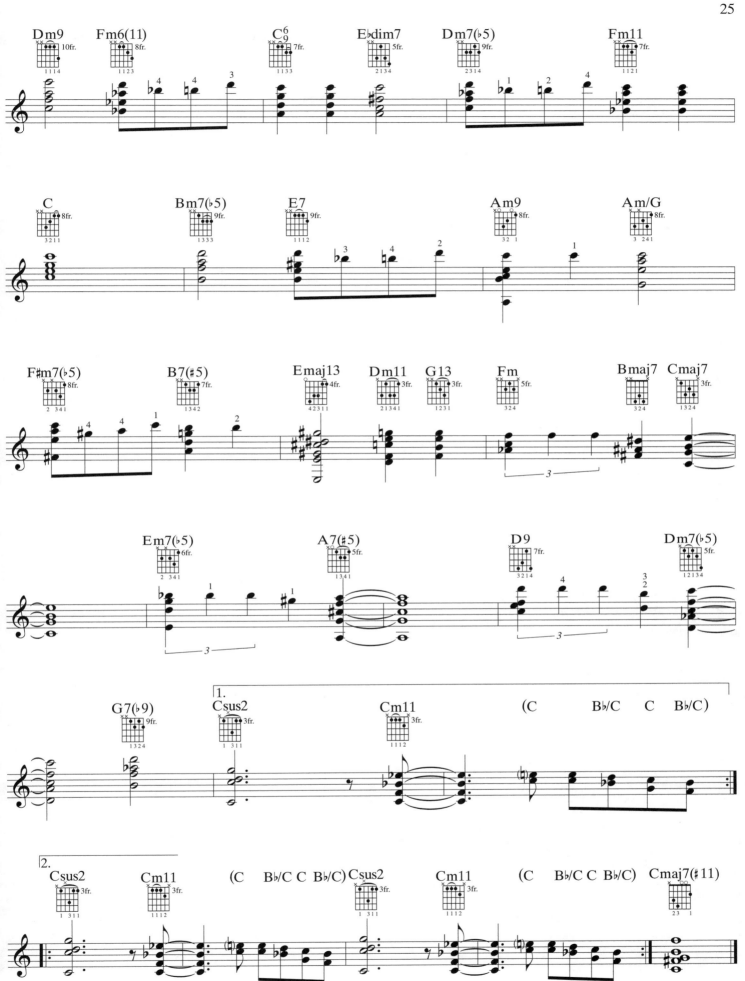

APRIL IN PARIS
(Solo)

Words by E. Y. HARBURG
Music by VERNON DUKE

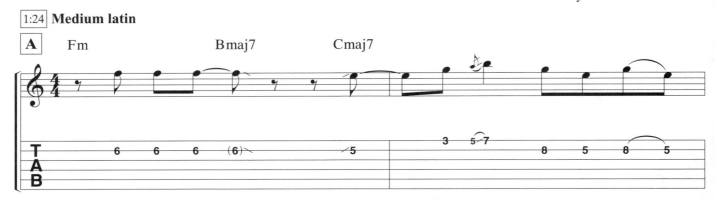

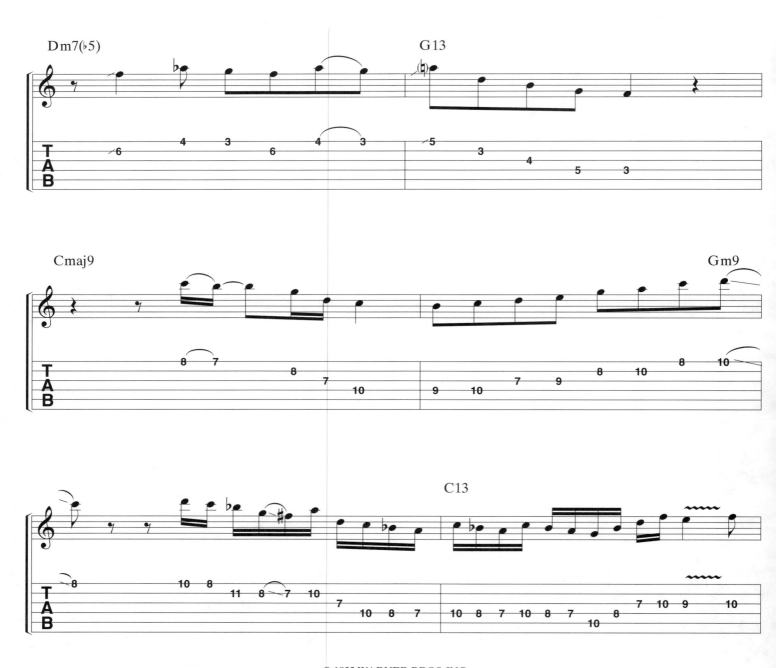

© 1932 WARNER BROS. INC.
Rights for the Extended Renewal Term in the United States Controlled by
GLOCCA MORRA MUSIC and KAY DUKE MUSIC
All Rights Reserved

0615B

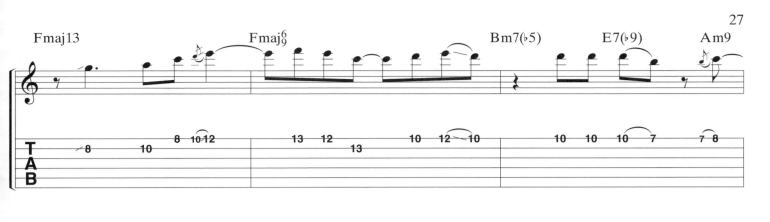

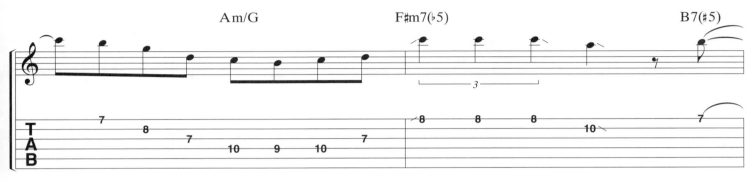

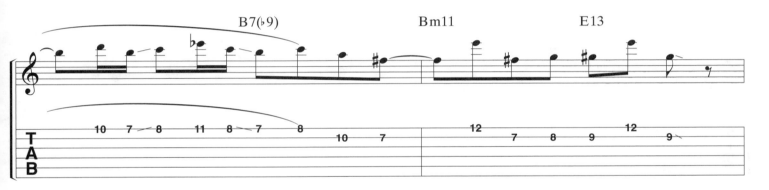

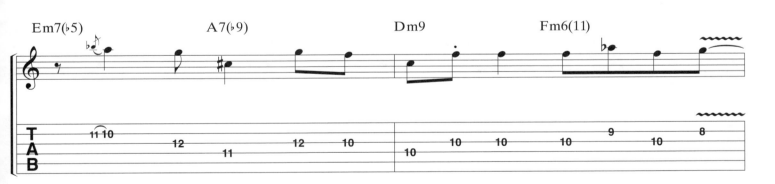

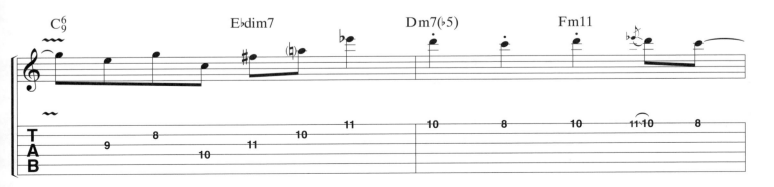

0615B

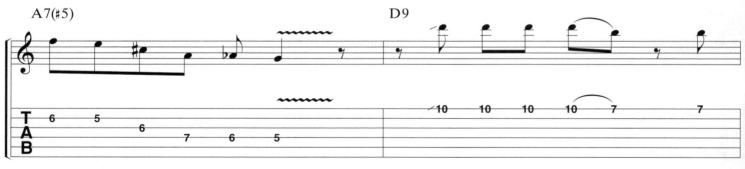

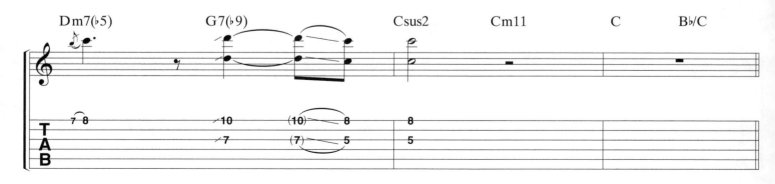

APRIL IN PARIS
(Original Fakebook Version)

Words by E. Y. HARBURG
Music by VERNON DUKE

© 1932 WARNER BROS. INC.
Rights for the Extended Renewal Term in the United States Controlled by
GLOCCA MORRA MUSIC and KAY DUKE MUSIC
All Rights Reserved

0615B

Just Friends

I first heard this song on guitarist Pat Martino's first recording, "Hombre." It's a great version to check out!

This song is definitely challenging for the soloist because it makes some treacherous turns. Bar 3 has a B♭ minor to an E♭7. You might think you're going to A♭, but the progression actually goes to F major—a definite twist. Now you're in F major and you might think that it's going to F minor, but instead it goes to A♭ minor. Then in bars 7 and 8, the II-V might lead you to G♭ major, but instead you go down a half step to G minor (from the A♭m–D♭7).

This kind of progression definitely keeps you on your toes, especially since it moves along at higher tempos. It's a great song to work out on and practice!

The Song

- This song has a 32-bar A-A1 form. Each section is 16 bars long.
- This version is in the key of B♭ major as opposed to the original, which is in C major.
- The A section stays around B♭ major but has two deceptive cadences (the B♭m7-E♭7 in bars 3 and 4, and the A♭m7-D♭7 in bars 7 and 8).
- The last four bars of the A section have a dominant VI chord (G7), which provides the necessary tension to push back to the top for the A1 section. This G7 can also feel like a secondary dominant II7 chord of the temporary tonal center of F major.
- The second half of the song (A1) is very similar to the first half except that the harmony and melody push to resolution two bars before the end (in this case F major).

The Solo

- This solo has barely a hint of the melody (beat 1 of bar 3 in the A section).
- There is a wide variety of phrase lengths that allow the solo to breath and swing.
- The sixteenth bar of the A section is a nice example of two chords connecting via their guide tones. The 7th of the Cm7 chord (B♭) connects to the 3rd of the F7 chord (A).
- There is a nice intervallic line starting in bar 5 of the A1 section that uses combinations of 5ths and 4ths in a sequential pattern.

Selected Recordings

Chet Baker, *Best of Chet Baker Sings,* EMD/Blue Note, 1953.

John Coltrane, *Coltrane Time,* EMD/Blue Note, 1958.

Tal Farlow, *Cookin' on All Burners,* Concord Jazz, 1982.

Claire Fischer, *Jazz Song,* Revelation, 1973:

    Claire Fisher (solo piano).

Wynton Marsalis, *Live at Blues Alley,* CBS, 1986:

    Wynton Marsalis (trumpet), Marcus Roberts (piano), Robert Hurst
    (bass), Jeff "Tain" Watts (drums).

Benedetto Renaissance Series "Il Palissandro," photo by John Bender, courtesy of Cindy Benedetto

JUST FRIENDS
(Chord-Melody Solo)

Music by JOHN KLENNER
Lyric by SAM M. LEWIS

* A pedal in bass throughout Intro.

© 1931 (Renewed 1959) METRO-GOLDWYN-MAYER, INC.
All Rights Controlled by EMI ROBBINS CATALOG INC. (Publishing) and WARNER BROS. PUBLICATIONS U.S. INC. (Print)
All Rights Reserved

JUST FRIENDS
(Solo)

Music by JOHN KLENNER
Lyric by SAM M. LEWIS

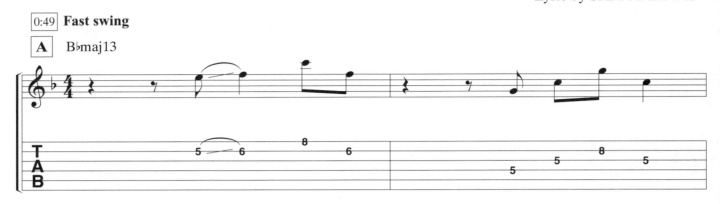

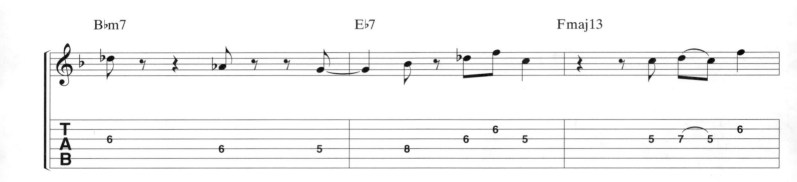

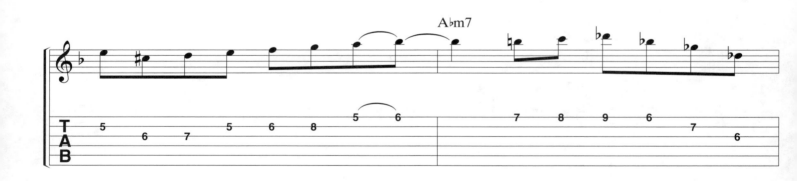

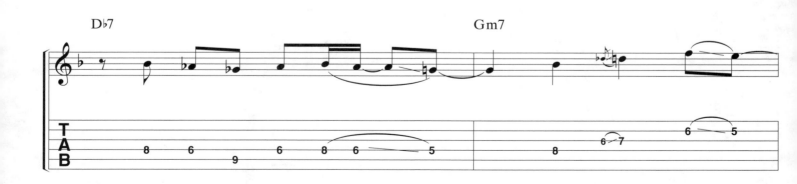

© 1931 (Renewed 1959) METRO-GOLDWYN-MAYER, INC.
All Rights Controlled by EMI ROBBINS CATALOG INC. (Publishing) and WARNER BROS. PUBLICATIONS U.S. INC. (Print)
All Rights Reserved

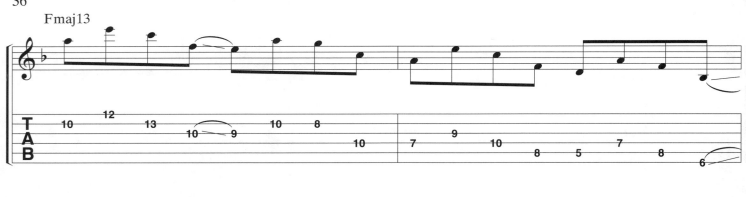

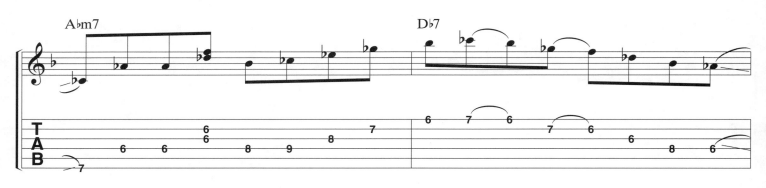

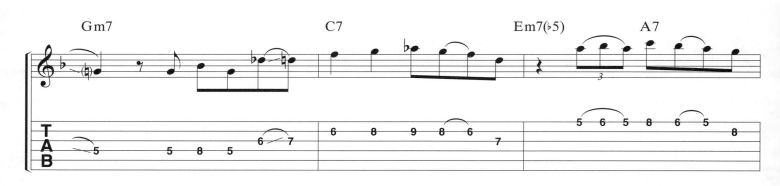

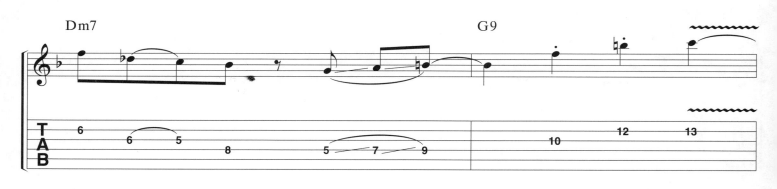

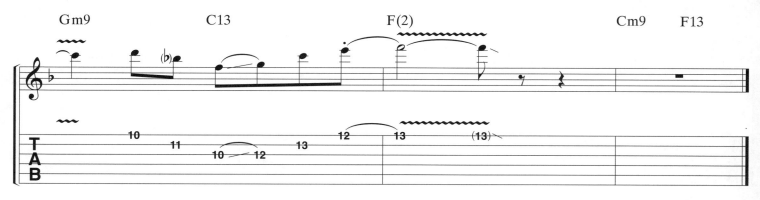

JUST FRIENDS
(Original Fakebook Version)

Music by JOHN KLENNER
Lyric by SAM M. LEWIS

© 1931 (Renewed 1959) METRO-GOLDWYN-MAYER, INC.
All Rights Controlled by EMI ROBBINS CATALOG INC. (Publishing) and WARNER BROS. PUBLICATIONS U.S. INC. (Print)
All Rights Reserved

0615B

Love Is Here to Stay

This song appeared in the motion picture *The Goldwyn Follies* in 1938. We took an unusual approach to this one by performing it in a 6/4 polyrhythmic groove instead of the usual 4/4 meter. This made the song somewhat more challenging to play and allowed us to explore some unusual rhythmic elements.

It's a simple song to solo over, but you should watch out for the E♭9(♭5). Try using the B♭ melodic minor scale here. The changes and chord voicings I used are common for the most part. There are many II-V's in the song; they should make it easier to solo over. During the head section, the progression going from E♭7(♭5)–D9–Bm7(♭5)–E7(♭9) might be the most difficult. I try to pick out the notes that define the chord and then land on those. For example, the line A–F♯–F–G♯ would be the ♭5–3rd–♭5–3rd of this chord progression. I might work on B♭ melodic minor, G major, C major, and A harmonic minor or B diminished scales, which also work over these chords. Practice playing over different II-V progressions to help you become more familiar with them.

The Song

- This song has a 32-bar A-A1 form. Each section is 16 bars long.
- The song is in the key of F major, but it starts on a dominant II chord (G7).
- The last four bars of the A section are briefly in D minor (relative minor of F major) but quickly cycle back to the dominant II chord (G7) for the next section.
- The last three bars of the A1 section differ from the A section in that they push to the tonic (F major) before setting up the return to the top (Am7 and D7 taking us to the G7 chord in bar 1).

The Solo

- This solo does something interesting in that it quotes from the melody, but only in a rhythmic sense (for example, bar 2 in the A section and bar 1 in the A1 section).
- Displaced eighth and quarter notes are phrased against the 6/4 meter throughout the solo.
- The solo is quite intervallic, which adds an angular feel to the odd meter and rhythmic devices in use.
- The solo ends with an interesting displaced quarter-note triplet figure (starting in bar 11).

Gibson "Le Grand," courtesy Gibson USA

Selected Recordings

Bill Evans, *Trio '65,* UNI/Verve, 1965:
    With Larry Bunker and Chuck Isreals.
Ella Fitzgerald and Louis Armstrong, *Our Love Is Here to Stay,* compilation-
    reissue UNI/Verve, 1998.
Stan Getz, *West Coast Jazz,* UNI/Verve, 1955.
Oscar Peterson, *Gershwin Songbooks,* UNI/Verve, 1952.

LOVE IS HERE TO STAY
(Chord-Melody Solo)

Music and Lyrics by
GEORGE GERSHWIN
and IRA GERSHWIN

© 1938 (Renewed 1965) GEORGE GERSHWIN MUSIC and IRA GERSHWIN MUSIC
All Rights Administered by WB MUSIC CORP.
All Rights Reserved

LOVE IS HERE TO STAY
(Solo)

Music and Lyrics by
GEORGE GERSHWIN
and **IRA GERSHWIN**

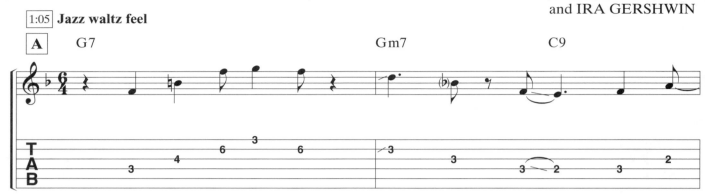

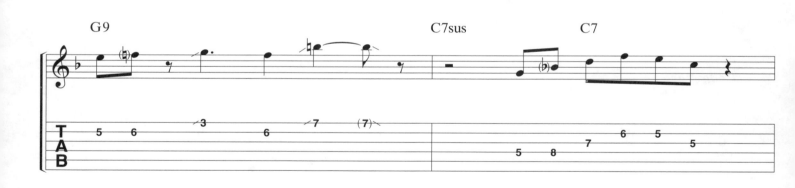

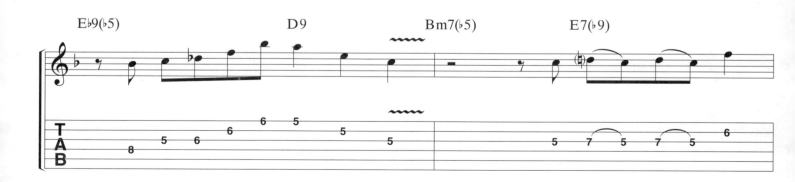

© 1938 (Renewed 1965) GEORGE GERSHWIN MUSIC and IRA GERSHWIN MUSIC
All Rights Administered by WB MUSIC CORP.
All Rights Reserved

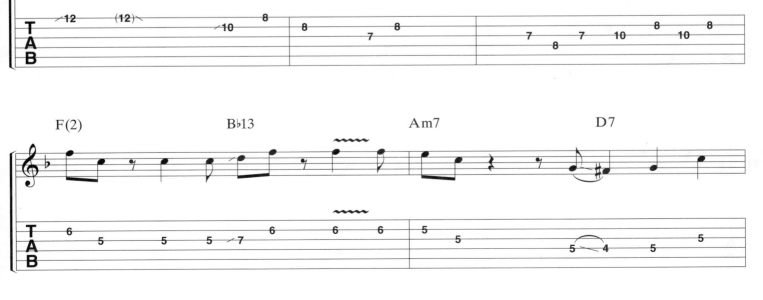

0615B

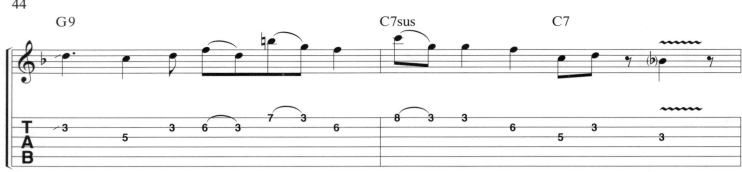

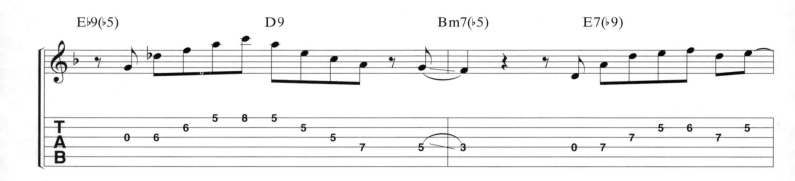

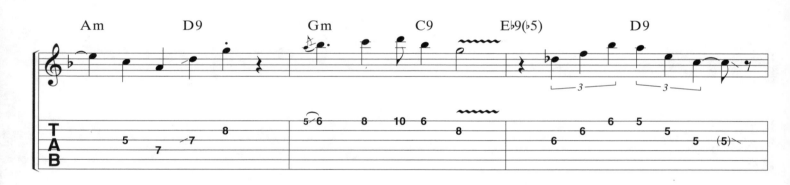

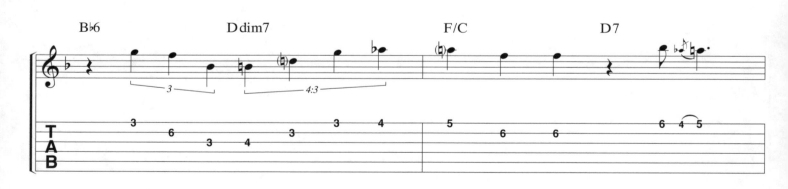

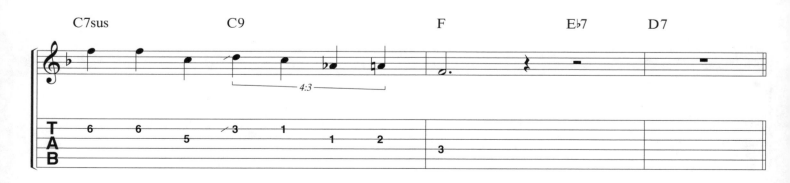

LOVE IS HERE TO STAY
(Original Fakebook Version)

Music and Lyrics by
GEORGE GERSHWIN
and IRA GERSHWIN

© 1938 (Renewed 1965) GEORGE GERSHWIN MUSIC and IRA GERSHWIN MUSIC
All Rights Administered by WB MUSIC CORP.
All Rights Reserved

A Day in the Life of a Fool

Composed by Brazilian guitarist Luiz Bonfá, this song appeared in the score of a 1958 film entitled *Black Orpheus*. This beautiful song has a haunting melody and is also known as "Manha de Carnaval." The melody fits very nicely in A minor. Use A minor and C major for soloing over this song form.

This song has a nice descending bass line at the bridge: Dm7–Dm/C–Bm7(♭5)–E7(♭9)–Am–Am/G–Fmaj7–Bm7–E7. The ending melody is a very nice part of the song. Here, I change the harmony slightly. You can try using the A harmonic minor scale on the E7th chords. You can also use the F melodic minor scale on this chord. The dominant 7th(♭5) chords can use the melodic minor scale starting a half step above the root of the chord. Did you notice the use of tritone substitution in the chord changes of this song [A♭7(♭5) and G♭7(♭5)]?

The Song

- This song has a 32-bar A–A1 form. Each section is 16 bars long.
- The song is in the key of A minor but moves to the relative major (C major) in bar 7.
- The last four bars of the A section work back to A minor (Bm7♭5–E7–Am7–E7) to set up the A1 section.
- The A1 section is the same as the A section for the first four bars. The A1 section then goes to the key of D minor (in bar 5) and then works its way nicely through a series of II-V's back to the home key of A minor.

The Solo

- The solo is quite arpeggio-oriented in nature and uses the A natural minor as well as harmonic minor scale (the G♯ in bar 4).
- There are some blues turns in bars 9 and 13 of the A section.
- There is a small reference to the original melody in bar 14.
- The solo ends with an interesting sixteenth-note riff using the open first string (bar 14 of the A1 section).

Selected Recordings

Luiz Bonfá, *The Bonfá Magic*, 1991:
    Luiz Bonfá (guitar).

Paul Desmond, *Live*, Horizon/A&M:
    Paul Desmond (alto), Ed Bickert (guitar), Don Thompson (bass), Jeffery Fuller (drums).

Vince Guaraldi, *Greatest Hits*, Fantasy:
    Vince Guaraldi (piano).

Benedetto "Benny" (Natural), photo by John Bender, courtesy of Cindy Benedetto

A DAY IN THE LIFE OF A FOOL
(Manha de Carnaval)
(Chord-Melody Solo)

Words by CARL SIGMAN
Music by LUIZ BONFA

© 1959 by NOUVELLES EDITIONS MERIDIAN
© 1964 by ANNE-RACHEL MUSIC CORP. and UNITED ARTISTS MUSIC CO., INC.
Copyrights Renewed
All Rights Administered by CHAPPELL & CO.
All Rights Reserved

0615B

A DAY IN THE LIFE OF A FOOL
(Manha de Carnaval)
(Solo)

Words by CARL SIGMAN
Music by LUIZ BONFA

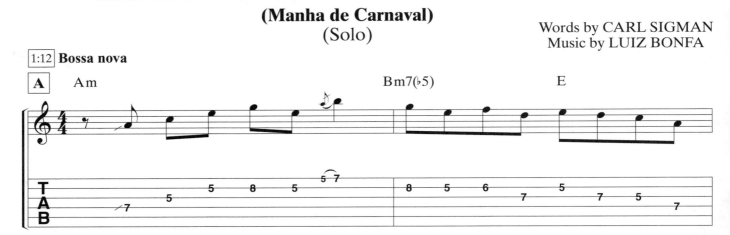

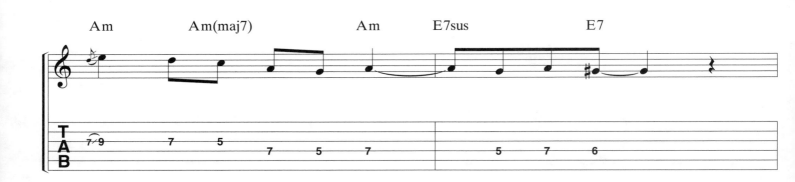

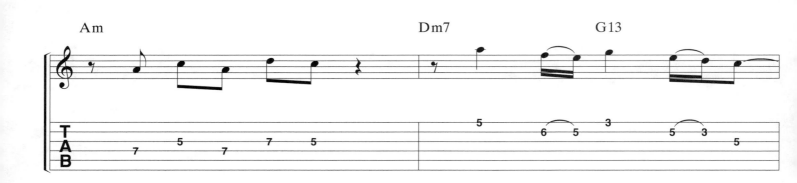

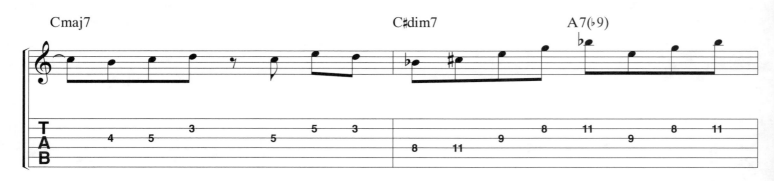

© 1959 by NOUVELLES EDITIONS MERIDIAN
© 1964 by ANNE-RACHEL MUSIC CORP. and UNITED ARTISTS MUSIC CO., INC.
Copyrights Renewed
All Rights Administered by CHAPPELL & CO.
All Rights Reserved

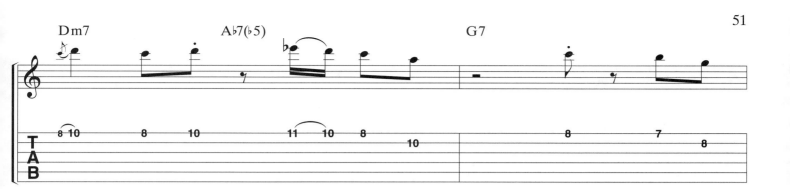

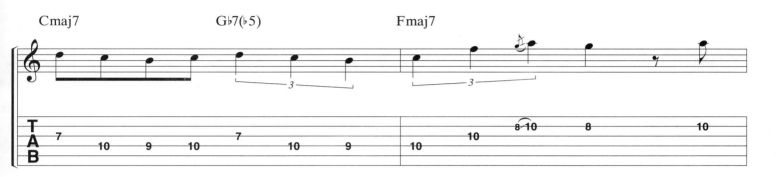

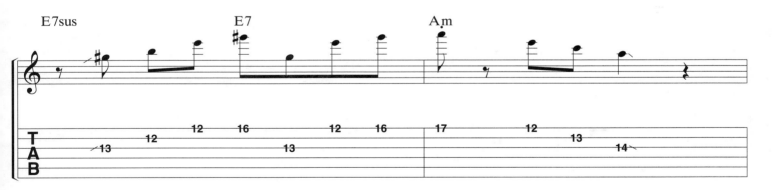

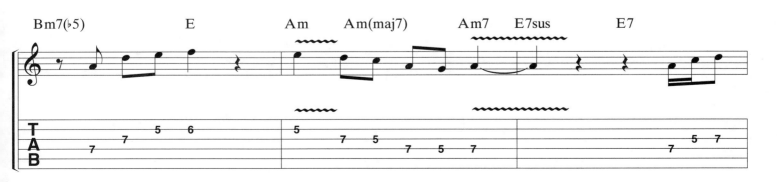

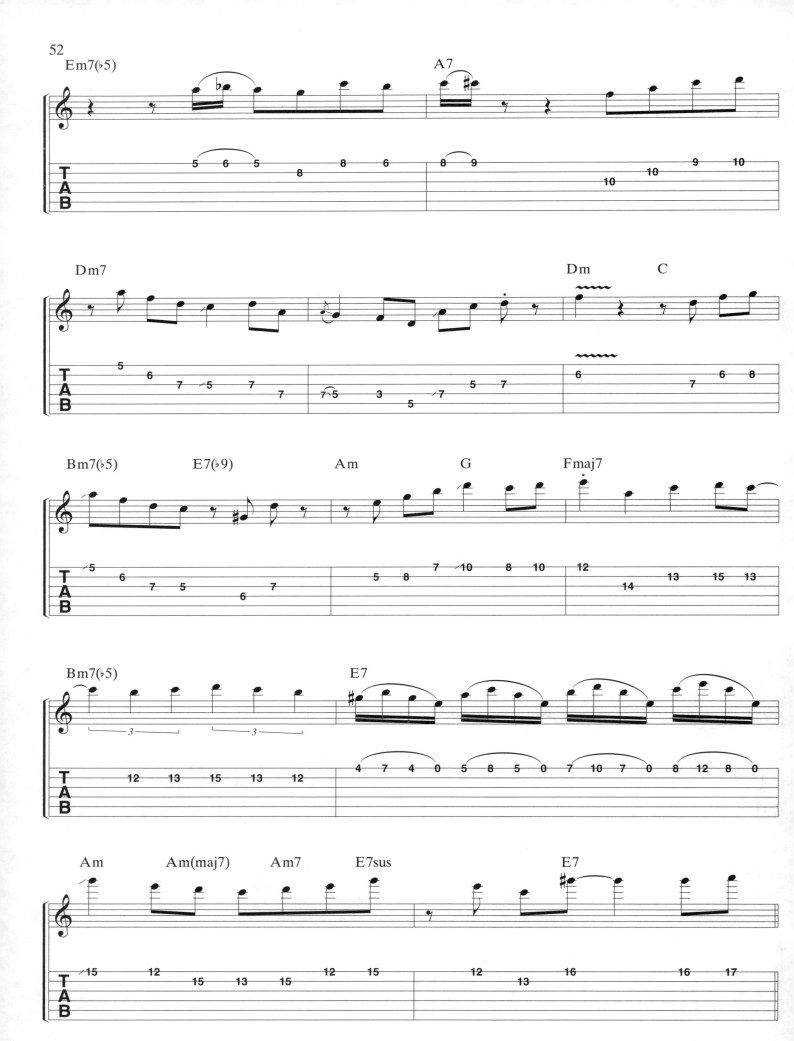

A DAY IN THE LIFE OF A FOOL
(Manha de Carnaval)
(Original Fakebook Version)

Words by CARL SIGMAN
Music by LUIZ BONFA

© 1959 by NOUVELLES EDITIONS MERIDIAN
© 1964 by ANNE-RACHEL MUSIC CORP. and UNITED ARTISTS MUSIC CO., INC.
Copyrights Renewed
All Rights Administered by CHAPPELL & CO.
All Rights Reserved

0615B

Misty

This song was the subject of the suspenseful 1971 Clint Eastwood-directed film *Play Misty for Me*. The song has a classic chord progression that moves logically through the key centers of E♭ major, A♭ major, G♭ major, and back to E♭ major. The bridge then goes to A♭ major, then to G major, and back to E♭ major.

For soloing, you can definitely start by using the corresponding major scales with each chord, and of course you have the melody as a template to use anywhere during your solo.

You'll find a great version of this song on guitarist Wes Montgomery's *The Complete Smokin' at the Half Note*, Vol. 2 recording with Wynton Kelly on piano, Paul Chambers on bass, and Jimmy Cobb on drums. Volume 1 is a very cool recording to add to your collection as well.

The Song

- This song has a 32-bar AABA form. Each section is eight bars long.
- The first A section is in the key of E♭ major but immediately modulates to the key of the IV chord (A♭ major) in bar 2. The IV chord then goes minor and moves in cycle to its V chord (D♭7) and then back to the home key of E♭. This is called a back-door II-V-I.
- The difference between the first two A sections is in their last two bars. The first A section doesn't resolve to the one chord (E♭), but the second A section does.
- The B section starts with a II-V into the key of the IV chord (A♭ major).
- In bar 5 of the B section, the harmony takes an unexpected turn to A minor and then beautifully cycles its way back to set up the last A section.
- The last A section can be like the second A section if you are ending the song, or the first A section if you are going back to the top for solos.

The Solo

- The solo has a scalar, bluesy feel to it from the start (bars 1 and 2).
- This feel continues throughout the solo with some nice across-the-barline runs (for example, bars 6 and 7 of the first A section).
- Arpeggios are used rather sparingly but with strong harmonic impact (bar 4).
- There are a lot of triplet phrases used to propel the solo. (The strongest example is found in bar 8 of the first A section and into the first three bars of the second A section.)

Gibson "Pat Martino" model, courtesy of Gibson USA

Selected Recordings

Wes Montgomery, *The Complete Smokin' at the Half Note,* Vol. 2, Verve, 1965.

Richard "Groove" Holmes, *Misty,* Fantasy Original Jazz Classics, 1965:
    Gene Edwards (guitar), George Randall (drums).

Duke Ellington, Ella Fitzgerald, and Coleman Hawkins, *The Greatest Jazz Concert in the World*, Fantasy/Pablo, 1975.

Barney Kessel, *Barney Kessel,* compilation, Giants of Jazz ITA, 1999.

MISTY
(Chord-Melody Solo)

Words by JOHNNY BURKE
Music by ERROLL GARNER

© 1954, 1955 (Copyrights Renewed) REGANESQUE MUSIC, MARKE MUSIC PUBLISHING CO., INC.,
LIMERICK MUSIC CORP., TIMO-CO MUSIC and OCTAVE MUSIC PUBLISHING CORP.
All Rights Reserved

MISTY
(Solo)

Words by JOHNNY BURKE
Music by ERROLL GARNER

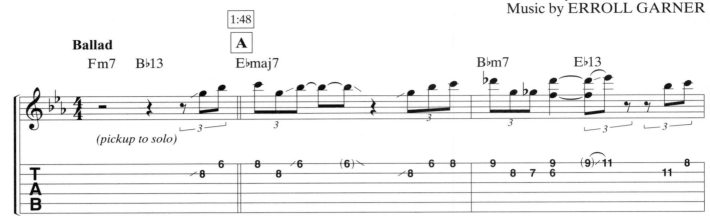

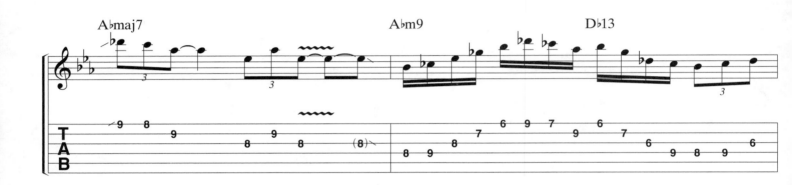

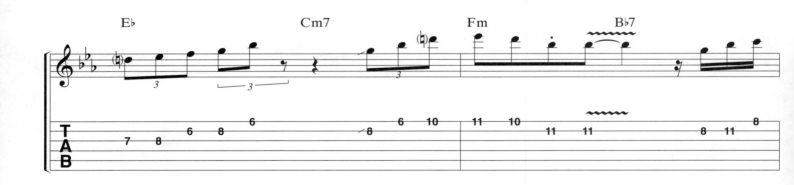

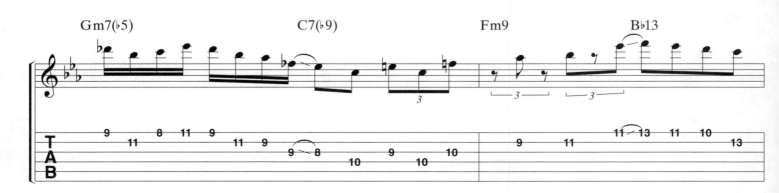

© 1954, 1955 (Copyrights Renewed) REGANESQUE MUSIC, MARKE MUSIC PUBLISHING CO., INC.,
LIMERICK MUSIC CORP., TIMO-CO MUSIC and OCTAVE MUSIC PUBLISHING CORP.
All Rights Reserved

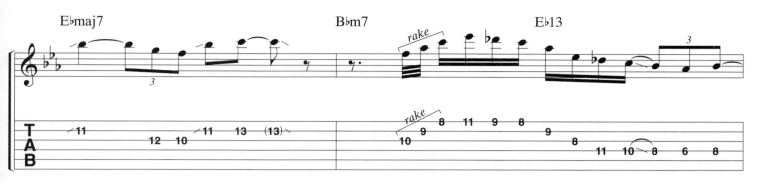

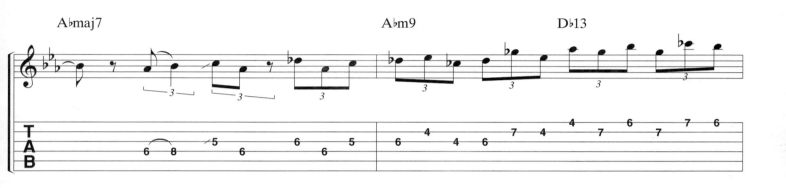

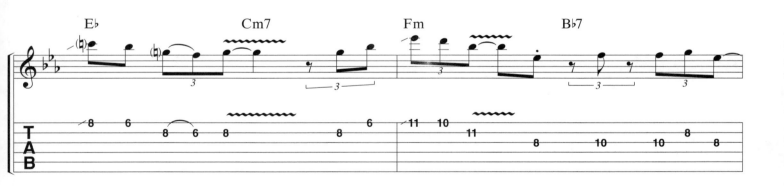

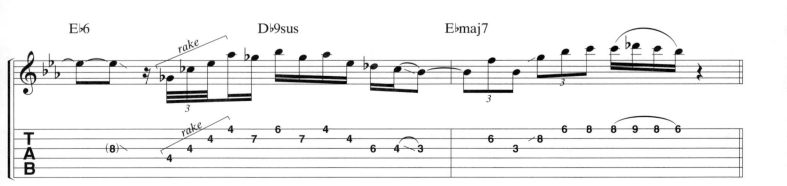

MISTY
(Original Fakebook Version)

Words by JOHNNY BURKE
Music by ERROLL GARNER

© 1954, 1955 (Copyrights Renewed) REGANESQUE MUSIC, MARKE MUSIC PUBLISHING CO., INC.,
LIMERICK MUSIC CORP., TIMO-CO MUSIC and OCTAVE MUSIC PUBLISHING CORP.
All Rights Reserved

My Foolish Heart

On this arrangement I used the basic standard chord voicings throughout except for the Cmaj7/F and the E♭13(#11). Also the Em11, Am9, and Cmaj7 at the end of the song in the turnaround are not common voicings. This song has a long chord progression but stays mainly in the key of C. I have also played this song as a bossa, and it worked nicely.

You have to hear Bill Evans' version on *The Bill Evans Trio At the Village Vanguard*. It was also included on Bill Evans' studio recording *Waltz for Debbie*, which was released a year or two later. It's a must-have for anyone's collection!

The Song

- This song has a 32-bar A-A1 form. Each section is 16 bars long.
- This version is in the key of C major, and the original is in the key of B♭ major.
- The song is harmonically clever. The harmony is essentially diatonic to C major, with the scale tone chords becoming temporary tonal centers due to their approach by II-V's. (For example, in bar 2 the Em7 to A7 set up the II chord, Dm7, to feel like a I chord in the key of D minor.) This happens throughout the piece (virtually every non-diatonic bar is some kind of II-V move).
- The last eight bars of the two sections differ in their respective pushes to the I chord (C major).

The Solo

- The solo is sparse and reflective as is the original melody of the song.
- In bar 3 of the A section is a sixteenth-note line that is played in groups of four notes, with the first grouping having only three notes. This helps make the accents fall off of the beat.
- Another interesting thing here is the use of the root of the chord as the first note of a line (for example, bars 2, 3, and 6 of the first A section. Louis Armstrong played on the root with great effect. So did Miles Davis and many jazz greats.

Selected Recordings

Bill Evans, *Waltz for Debbie*, JVC Victor import.

Bill Evans Trio, *At the Village Vanguard*, Riverside, 1961.

Oscar Peterson, *Tribute: Live at Town Hall*, TelArc, 1997.

Sonny Stitt, *Deuces Wild*, Collectable Records, 1966.

MY FOOLISH HEART
(Chord-Melody Solo)

Words by NED WASHINGTON
Music by VICTOR YOUNG

© 1949 CHAPPELL & CO.
Copyright Renewed and Assigned to CHAPPELL & CO. and CATHERINE HINEN
All Rights Reserved

MY FOOLISH HEART
(Solo)

Words by NED WASHINGTON
Music by VICTOR YOUNG

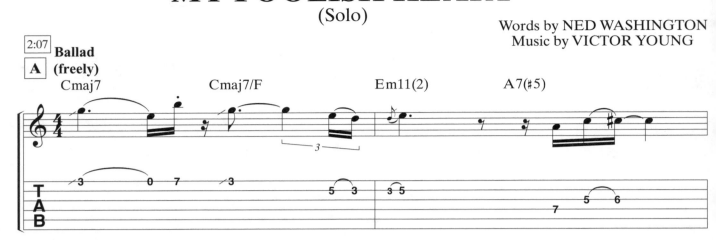

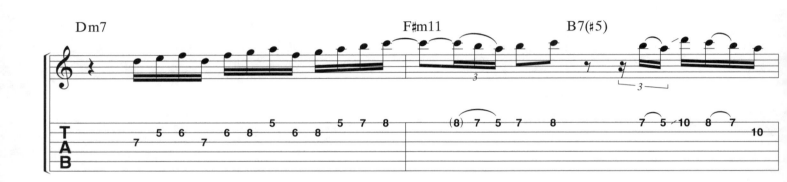

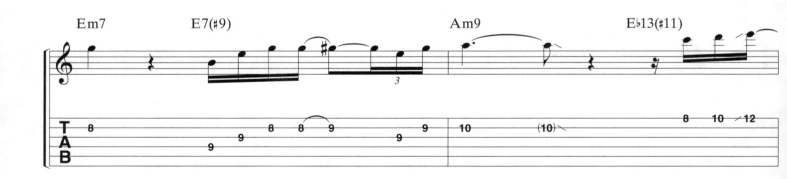

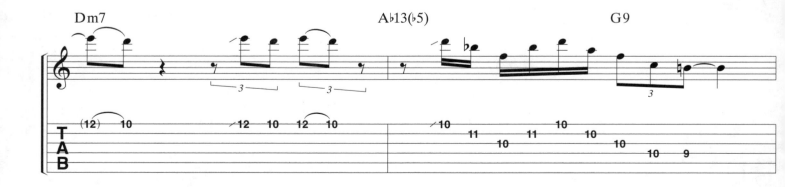

© 1949 CHAPPELL & CO.
Copyright Renewed and Assigned to CHAPPELL & CO. and CATHERINE HINEN
All Rights Reserved

0615B

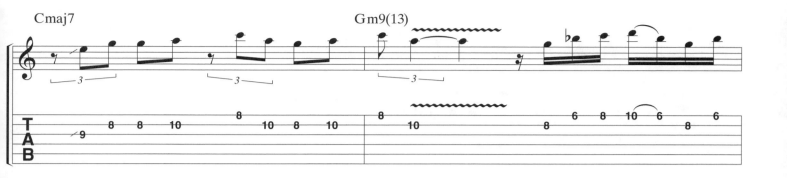

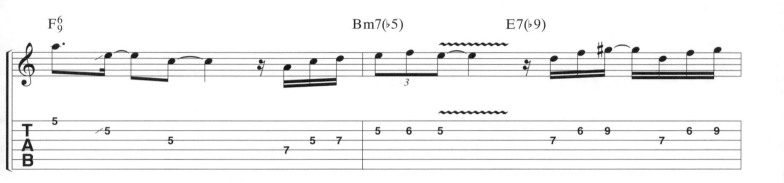

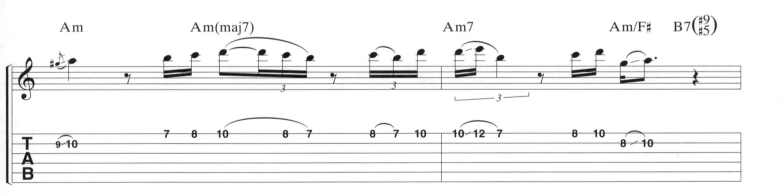

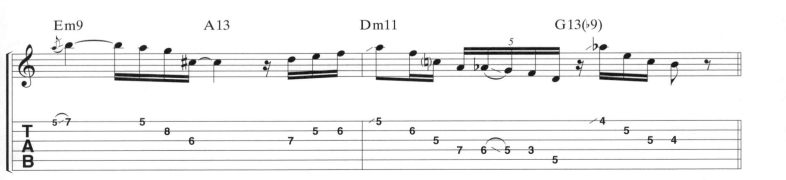

0615B

MY FOOLISH HEART
(Original Fakebook Version)

Words by NED WASHINGTON
Music by VICTOR YOUNG

© 1949 CHAPPELL & CO.
Copyright Renewed and Assigned to CHAPPELL & CO. and CATHERINE HINEN
All Rights Reserved

Andersen "Streamline," courtesy of Steve Andersen, Andersen Guitars

Autumn in New York

This beautiful ballad is maybe a lesser-known standard. I stayed close to basic traditional chord voicings but still took a few liberties here with some substitutions. Check out the G13/F and the Cm11. Also take a look at the E♭sus and the F13sus at the end of the piece. These changes add more color and texture as compared to the more traditional chord voicings and give the soloist more choices melodically.

For soloing, check out the F major scale, but also try to catch some of the altered notes in the dominant chord voicings (3rd, 7th, ♭9th). It's a long form to solo over, so start out slow and easy because you have plenty of time to build your solo—something to think about on any solo.

Take your time to develop your statement as a soloist, and listen to the other musicians. Developing a conversation between you and the other musicians can greatly improve a solo.

The Song

- This song has a 32 bar A-A1 form. Each section is 16 bars long.
- In the seventh bar of the A1 section is an extra chord on beat 3 (A♭m9) that doesn't appear in the original version.
- The A section starts on the II chord in the key of F major (Gm7) and proceeds to walk up the scale tone chords to the V and then back to the I chord (F major).
- In the next four bars the same thing starts to happen, but there is a resolution to the III chord (Am).
- The next four bars see a move to A♭ major, and the last four bars of the A section end on a dominant posture in the key of F major (C7).
- The first four bars of the A1 section are the same as the first section, but then things take some interesting harmonic moves through some II-V's, ending up in B♭ minor.
- The A1 section ends interestingly in F minor.

The Solo

- The solo is composed of mostly triplet figures of eighth and sixteenth notes.
- Bars 5 and 6 of the A section show the use of broken triplets to create rhythmic tension.
- Bars 11 and 12 of the A section have a series of sixteenth-note triplets.
- The A1 section starts with a distant quote of the melody, with it again stated more strongly in bar 13.
- There are some blues lines in the A1 section in bars 8 and 15.

Gibson "Howard Roberts" model, courtesy of Gibson US

- A brief use of double-stops (two notes played at once) occurs in the same section in bar 14.

Selected Recordings

Chet Baker, *Art of the Ballad: Chet Baker,* 1958.

Kenny Burrell, *Blue Lights,* Vol.1, EMI/Blue Note import.

Clifford Brown, *The Complete Emarcy Record,* UNI/Verve, 1954.

Tal Farlow, *Autumn in New York,* Verve, 1954:

    Tal Farlow (guitar), Gerry Wiggins (piano), Ray Brown (bass), Chico Hamilton (drums).

Ahmad Jamal, *Ahmad's Blues,* UNI GRP, 1958:

    Ahmed Jamal (piano), Israel Crosby (bass), Vernel Fournier (drums).

AUTUMN IN NEW YORK
(Chord-Melody Solo)

Words and Music by
VERNON DUKE

© 1934 WARNER BROS. INC.
Rights for the Extended Renewal Term in the United States Controlled by
KAY DUKE MUSIC (c/o BMG SONGS INC.)
All Rights Reserved   Used by Permission

AUTUMN IN NEW YORK
(Solo)

Words and Music by
VERNON DUKE

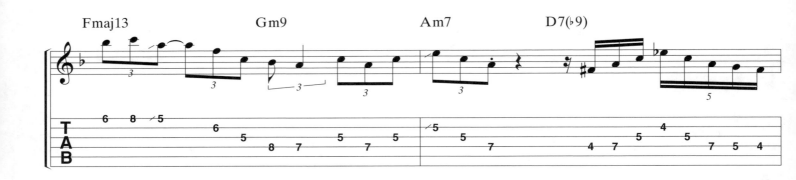

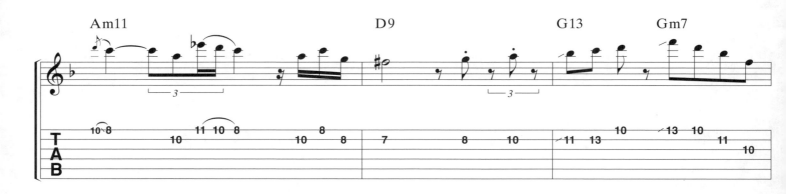

© 1934 WARNER BROS. INC.
Rights for the Extended Renewal Term in the United States Controlled by
KAY DUKE MUSIC (c/o BMG SONGS INC.)
All Rights Reserved   Used by Permission

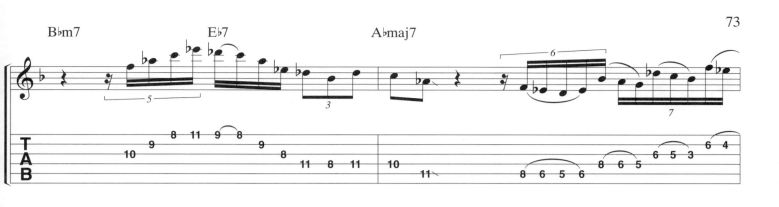

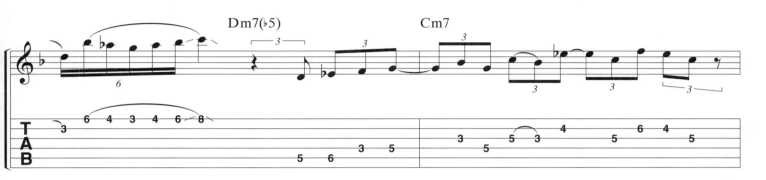

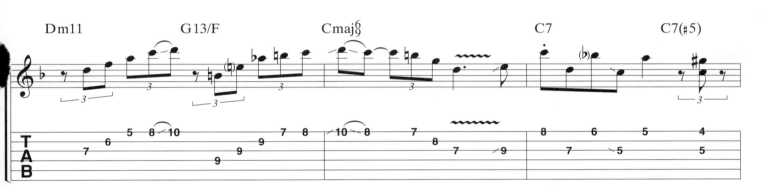

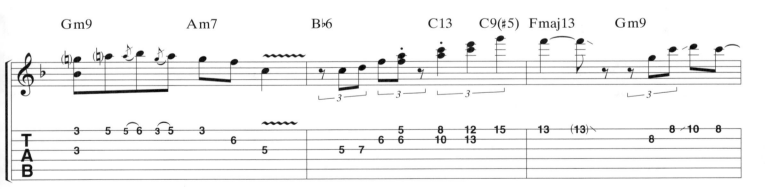

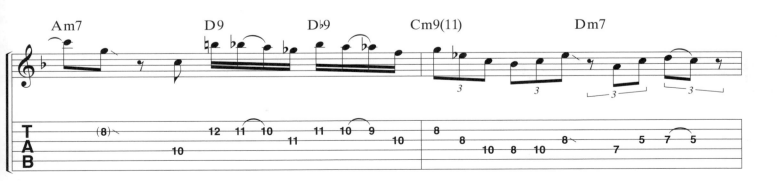

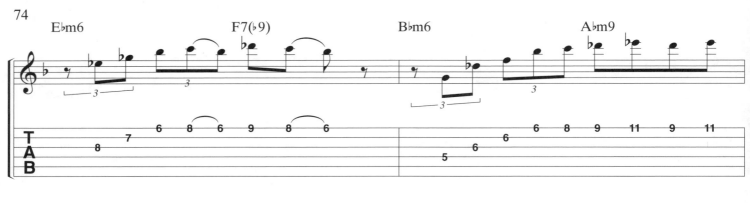

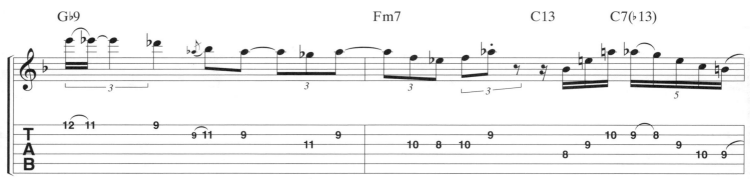

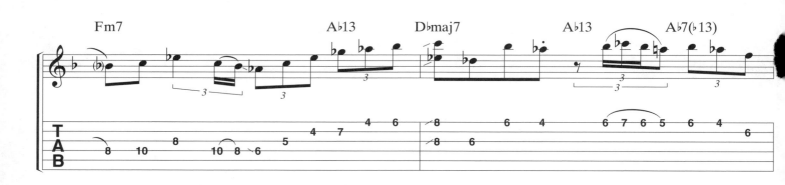

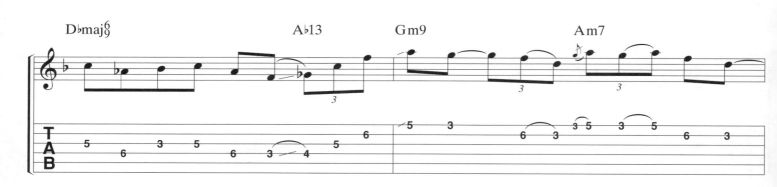

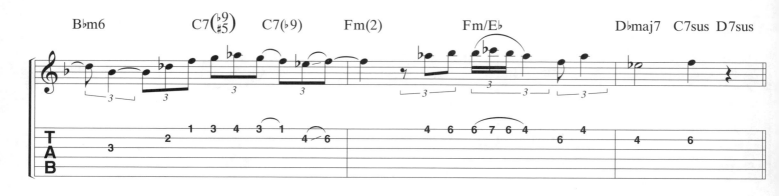

AUTUMN IN NEW YORK
(Original Fakebook Version)

Words and Music by
VERNON DUKE

© 1934 WARNER BROS. INC.
Rights for the Extended Renewal Term in the United States Controlled by
KAY DUKE MUSIC (c/o BMG SONGS INC.)
All Rights Reserved   Used by Permission

THE BEST IN *Jazz*

The *Just Real Book* Series

The most complete and accurate fakebook series of all time.

Each fakebook in the *Just Real Book* series contains hundreds of songs that are the core repertoire for musicians all over the world. Original composer sources were consulted to ensure that the arrangements remained true to the composers' intention. Plus, useful and important chord substitutions are indicated for each arrangement. Each book is extensively cross-referenced with appendices including: a complete composer index, a complete discography, a section on how to play from a fakebook, chord theory reference pages, and a section on how to create interesting chord substitutions. Comb bound.

Just Standards Real Book

C Edition	(FBM0002)	$39.95
B♭ Edition	(FBM0002BF)	$39.95
E♭ Edition	(FBM0002EF)	$39.95

Just Jazz Real Book

C Edition	(FBM0003)	$39.95
B♭ Edition	(FBM0003BF)	$39.95
E♭ Edition	(FBM0003EF)	$39.95
Bass Clef Edition	(FBM0003BS)	$39.95

Just Blues Real Book

C Edition	(FBM0004)	$39.95

The *21st Century Pro Method* Series

The most complete method for the modern jazz guitarist.

Jazz Guitar—Swing to Bebop
Spiral-Bound Book and CD
(0388B) $24.95
This book covers music theory, scales, modes, chord voicings, arpeggios, soloing, and comping. More than 180 music examples and 16 complete solos in the styles of many jazz greats are used to place all concepts in the context of classic jazz chord progressions and standards. A CD with all the music examples is included!

Jazz Guitar—Bebop and Beyond
Spiral-Bound Book and CD
(0609B) $24.95
This book explores advanced, modern jazz and bebop concepts, and techniques, including music theory, scales, modes, chord voicings, arpeggios, soloing, and comping concepts. More than 170 music examples and 13 complete solos in the styles of many jazz greats are used to place all concepts into a practical musical context. A CD with all the music examples is included!

AD1087 7/02